LES
DAWSON's
JOKE
BOOK

LES DAWSON's JOKE BOOK

Compiled by
Tracy and Charlotte Dawson

MICHAEL O'MARA BOOKS LIMITED

First published in Great Britain in 2012 by
Michael O'Mara Books Limited
9 Lion Yard
Tremadoc Road
London SW4 7NQ

A CIP catalogue record for this book is available from the British Library.

Papers used by Michael O'Mara Books Limited are natural, recyclable
products made from wood grown in sustainable forests.
The manufacturing processes conform to the environmental regulations
of the country of origin.

ISBN: 978-1-84317-870-5 in hardback print format
ISBN: 978-1-84317-987-0 in EPub format
ISBN: 978-1-84317-988-7 in Mobipocket format

1 2 3 4 5 6 7 8 9 10

Designed by Design 23, London
Illustrations by Greg Stevenson

Printed and bound by CPI Group (UK) Ltd, Croydon, CR0 4YY

www.mombooks.com

Dedication

For all the people who loved Les throughout his
life and continue to keep his memory alive.

Contents

Introduction

by Tracy and Charlotte Dawson

Tracy
'You know Les Dawson?'

"Course. Comedian. Famous. Been dead a while, but you still find clips of him everywhere. And DVDs and stuff. Very funny man.'

'He was a writer.'

'Nah, he was a stand-up comic. Had his own TV shows for years. Good pianist, too, though he liked to mess about, playing bum notes and stuff.'

'Sure, but he was a writer too.'

'I didn't know that.'

That's an imaginary conversation, of course, but to paraphrase Michael Caine, not a lot of people know that. Writing was one of the great joys of Les's life, and he would spend hours in his study composing new gags, honing old ones and putting together new material for all his shows. Les left me a cupboard full of fabulously funny material, some typed, some handwritten, and said it was for our daughter Charlotte's legacy. There were sketches and opening spots, one-line gags and jottings of ideas for development – as well as some much longer works. He once made me promise to make sure that people knew he was a writer as well as a comedian, and I hope you agree that the following pages show off his talent in both departments brilliantly.

It's hard to believe it, but June 2013 marks twenty years since Les died. Twenty years! It is astonishing to me that he's been gone for so long. It is true that the really great comedians never die; you have only to think of Tony Hancock, Tommy Cooper, Eric Morecambe, Spike Milligan – and Les – to know that. But a part of the reason for his enduring appeal is that he's still so well loved: everyone still remembers him so fondly. And it's not just the 'older' generation either, for today's rising young comedians often cite Les as one of their comedy heroes, bringing him to a whole new generation of younger people.

Les put his whole life into making people laugh, and he absolutely loved his work. The phrase 'once seen, never forgotten' might have been coined for him, and that is true of his newer audience of people who have perhaps only ever seen him on DVDs or television repeats. His audiences – as well as people he passed daily in the street – warmed to him because he was just like them in many ways. His act was appealing because everyone felt as if they knew him personally. And that's why, when you read his jokes and patter, it's hard to do so without putting on his voice and hearing him tell them to you direct.

Charlotte

I was only tiny when my dad died but I know how much he loved me – and still does. Although I missed out on having him with me through my childhood, I do think I'm quite lucky in a way, as his legacy certainly lives on. I love watching him perform. I share his sense of humour and fun, and I can see why people love him so much after all these years – his humour is timeless. And, of course, lots of people – family, friends and strangers alike – have fantastic memories of him that they have shared with me over the years.

I'm really proud to be his daughter and I hope he's proud to know that I'm following in his footsteps into the world of entertainment.

This book – a collection of Les's jokes, stories and one-liners – sparkles with his humour. It cannot fail to bring a smile to all his fans – both those who knew Les during his life and those who have come to enjoy his humour over the last twenty years.

We hope you enjoy it as much as we enjoyed compiling it.

TRACY DAWSON
CHARLOTTE DAWSON

TAKE MY MOTHER-IN-LAW ...

I took the mother-in-law to Madame Tussauds Chamber of Horrors and one of the attendants said, 'Keep her moving, sir, we're stocktaking.'

She's so fat that when she passes her handbag from hand to hand she throws it.

She's so fat that when she went to the doctor for a check-up he said, 'I'll get the car out and have a look around you.'

The only success the mother-in-law ever had was with the council – selling her mince pie lids as manhole covers.

❀

I spent three weeks pushing a pan scrubber in the baby's face.
I want him to get used to kissing his grandmother.

❀

The mother-in-law – she's a sort of Third World War with knickers.

❀

When my mother-in-law smiled it looked like a crack across a septic tank.

Cooking

I'm not saying my mother-in-law is a rotten cook, but Fanny Craddock broke in the kitchen one night and welded her oven door up. Her gravy is so thick we call her the wizard of ooze. She did a chicken the other week and the only part you could chew was the beak. The father-in-law once got six months for stealing a car battery. He was worried because he has rheumatism. The judge said, 'Don't worry I'll put you in a dry cell' – which was an acid remark. Anyway, the mother-in-law went to visit him. He said, 'I'm going to escape. Bake a cake and put a file in it.'

When she came again he said, 'Next time, just bring a pickaxe and a steam hammer.'

'What's wrong with a file?' she asked.

'Nothing, but I can't get your bloody cake open!'

I've never seen eye to eye with the mother-in-law – not surprising, she's well over six foot – and what a size! When she stands in the nude she looks like a wall of whitewash. She's so fat she had to lose weight to model maternity frocks. She's the only woman I know who eats piranha fish – live. She never stops talking – she's got a fan belt fitted to her tongue.

She took the father-in-law to a psychiatrist. She said, 'There's something wrong with him, he never hears a word I say.'

The psychiatrist said, 'That's not an affliction – it's a bloody gift.'

It's been a rotten week, this. Four times at three o'clock in the morning a finger has poked me in the ear and a little voice whispered, 'Take me to the bathroom, please.'

I said to the wife yesterday, 'I'm fed up with this. It's time your mother went on her own now.'

All the mother-in-law talks about is how mean her husband is. When he found out he was going bald, rather than buy a wig, he changed his religion so he could wear a turban. I wouldn't say he's that mean, although he does keep an old-fashioned mangle out in the back yard to get the last kick from his toothpaste tubes.

I upset the wife's mother last Guy Fawkes
night.
I fell off the fire.

❋

She possessed all the charm only to be found
in a Tunisian culvert.

❋

My God, my mother-in-law can talk!
Still, you'd expect to find a long tongue in an
old boot.

❋

Wife: 'We're having mother for dinner.'
Me: 'Really? I'd prefer lamb.'

❋

I left the wife's mother in the car.
I'd have brought her in but I lost the keys to
the boot.

❀

During the War she was an Avon Lady. In
Colditz.

❀

She's getting too old to dye her hair properly
– remember the old saying 'only the good
dye young'?

❀

She has so many wrinkles that when she
smiles she looks like a Venetian blind.

❀

Cooking 2

I got home last night, the wife was in the kitchen. I knew she was getting my tea ready; I could hear the fire extinguisher going. Don't get me wrong, I'm not saying she's a rotten cook but when I bought her a hi-speed gas stove all I got was my toast burned in half the time. She once sent a recipe for rissoles to Jimmy Young and she got three months for posting a threatening letter.

Her mother's even worse – she has to spray her kitchen with DDT before the flies will come in. The wasps don't buzz around her bin, they lean on it and groan.

Her mother did me a meal last week. She called it Chicken a la Football Supporter. I don't know which team I got ... but I think it was Arsenal.

There's only one thing wrong ...

I'm often accused of saying some pretty rotten things about my mother-in-law. But quite honestly she's only got one major fault – it's called breathing. It's hard to describe what she looks like but she used to be a model for spanners. She's a hell of a size. When she crosses her legs it's like looking at two sides of bacon in a stranglehold . . . She hung her brassiere out on the line to dry the other day and a camel tried to make love to it . . . She's got more chins than a Chinese telephone directory.

Last week in Crewe she bent down and they had an eclipse in Burma. It's ridiculous, every time she hangs her knickers up people think we've painted the house. During the war the French wanted to give her a medal but they couldn't get a general to kiss her. I don't blame them. Her face has stopped so many clocks they've had to blindfold Big Ben.

My mother-in-law fell down a wishing well.
I was amazed. I never knew they worked.

She called me a thief, a coward, a rat, a
skunk and a liar.
I was blazing, because I'm not a liar.

***

The wife's mother's got so many gold teeth
she sleeps with her head in a strong box.

***

My mother-in-law gives such frosty looks
her glasses are double-glazed.

***

My mother-in-law went on holiday last
week.
The parrot thought he'd gone deaf.

Time's a great healer...

She came to live with us a month ago. I remember the day well – although time's a great healer. I'd woke up and was lay listening to the rent man digging a tunnel into the living room – he never gets paid round our way, he has to bring a violin and busk for his money. The wife was lay on her back fast asleep like a baby, with a big toe in her mouth. As usual she was wearing a mudpack. I'll never get used to it – she looks like quicksand with curlers . . .

Just then I heard a knock on the front door. I knew it was the wife's mother because the mice were putting cheese back on the traps and our cat had kittens – and he's a doctored tom. I opened the door before the paint peeled and there she was: Captain Birdseye with corsets. When she kissed me on the cheek it was like being attacked by an inner tube.

The wife came down. She said, 'Have you put the gas fire on in my mother's room?'

I said, 'Yes, but I've not lit it.'

The mother in law was at the rugby this
week – not staying – playing.

❀

Me and the wife were held up on our
honeymoon. They took everything.
The wife said, 'I saved our money and
camera by putting them in my mouth.'
I said, 'Pity your mother wasn't with us, we'd
have saved our suitcases.'

❀

The wife's mother said, 'When you're dead,
I'll dance on your grave.'
I said, 'Good. I'm being buried at sea.'

❀

My mother-in-law is kind – kind of fat and
baggy.

Cleopatra lay stretched out on the heaped Arabian pony skins, like a sensuous throbbing cat. As her handmaidens oiled her shimmering body she glowed in anticipation of seeing Antony, her lover.

The flickering pallid flame from the rush lights threw her tawny magnificence into bold relief against the wine-dark hides of the tent. Antony entered the scented dimness and, throwing aside his armour, he took her into his arms in a heated embrace – his masculine musk making heady her senses.

She whispered, 'Antony, my dear heart, let's not go out tonight – let's have a musical evening at home.'

'How mean you, angel?' said Antony, biting into a faggot sandwich.

'Well,' she said, 'I've booked a lute player from a working-men's club. And here's the first act.' She clapped her hands and a slave from Gaul was thrown onto the floor. He was drunk – definitely a Gaul stoned. Two naked Nubian eunuchs then wheeled a brass gong across his body.

And Cleopatra sang, 'I'm rolling a gong on the chest of a slave . . .'

❋

Mosquitoes draw straws to see who's going
to bite her.

❋

You can't give her a pinch – it's a handful or
nothing.

THE WIFE WAS FANNING HER MOTHER WITH A
KIPPER — I SAID USE USE CHEESE YOU FOOL
SHE SAID I'VE GOT TO GET THE BLOODY
CAT OUT FIRST..... THEY MAKE A FINE PAIR
THE WIFE AND HER MOTHER — ONE'S BANDY THE
OTHER'S KNOCKNEED ... WHEN THEY STAND UP TOGETHER
IN THE NUDE THEY SPELL OX ... THE WIFE
WOKE ME UP THE OTHER MORNING SHE SAID
THERE'S A BURGLAR DOWN STAIRS I SAID
WHATS HE DOING — SHE SAID HE'S SAT IN
THE KITCHEN EATING MY HOME MADE FRUIT
CAKE — SO I GOT BACK IN BED THE WIFE
SAID AREN'T YOU GOING FOR THE POLICE I
SAID NO NEED TO I'LL GO DOWN IN
THE MORNING AND BURY HIM.... WHAT
A COOK.... THE BLUE BOTTLES DON'T BUZZ
ROUND OUR DUSTBIN THEY LEAN ON IT
AND GROAN.... I'LL NEVER FORGET THE
DAY SHE TOSSED HER FIRST PANCAKE — WE'LL
NEVER KNOW WHAT SHE PUT IN THE MIXTURE
BUT FOR THE LAST SEVEN YEARS WE'VE
USED IT AS A PELMET..... YOU'VE NOT

Tomorrow it's the mother-in-law's funeral –
and she's cancelled it.

❋

She hasn't got vital statistics, just cubic
capacity.

❋

Crime

I was leaving the house the other morning and in
the front garden I saw the mother-in-law lying on
the rockery being attacked by six big fellows armed
with pickaxe handles.

The woman next door said, 'Aren't you going to
help?'

I said, 'Why should I? I don't know who started
it.'

She grabbed my arm and screamed down my
ear, 'Stop it before they batter her to pieces!' I was
instantly furious – if there's one thing I can't stand
it's anybody screaming down my ear.

But that incident highlights how serious crime

is today. The local bank got robbed last week. A masked gunman ran in – slipped on a banana skin. His gun went off, his mask fell off as he banged his head and his braces snapped as he lay on the floor. The bank manager said, 'Is this a hold up?' The fellow said, 'No, a cock up.'

The other night a youngster across the street shot his parents so he could go on an orphans' picnic. I've never seen kids like them – they go taking hubcaps off cars … while they're moving.

Last week a girl was raped by an idiot. I said, 'How do you know he was an idiot?'

The girl replied, 'I had to show him what to do.'

Violence is on the increase in this country. In some parts nuns have started going round with steel-tipped rosary beads.

The vicar at our local church asked a choirboy, 'Where is your daddy?' He responded, 'My daddy's gone up above.'

The vicar said gently, 'He's gone to heaven, my son.'

The lad said, 'No, he's taking the lead off the roof.'

Everybody's at it: a man from down the street came up to me on my way to the studio tonight and said, 'Stick 'em up.' I said, 'Stick what up?' and he said, 'I'm not sure, I'm new to this game.'

❋

I fed the mother-in-law arsenic with sun tan
lotion so she'd look good at the funeral.

My mother-in-law has come round to our
house at Christmas seven years running.
This year we're going to have a change. We're
going to let her in.

JUST FOR
A LAUGH

I stood entranced as he lightly fingered his crochets. He turned and when he saw me he whispered, 'It's Schubert.'
I said, 'It isn't, I smelt it when I came in.'

The service in restaurants gets worse. I said to one waiter, 'Do I sit here until I starve?'
He said, 'No, we shut the kitchens at six.'

Waxing lyrical

In awe I watched the waxing moon ride across the zenith of the heavens like an ambered chariot towards the ebony void of infinite space wherein the tethered belts of Jupiter and Mars hang, forever festooned in their orbital majesty. And as I looked at all this I thought ... I must put a roof on this lavatory.

I went to a guesthouse. The manager said,
'You want a room with running water?' I
said, 'What do you think I am, a trout?'

I had a car once, I called it Flattery because it
never got me anywhere. It was a Manchester
convertible – half car, half canoe. Six months
of the year it was a raft.

Picasso got run over the other day. He drew
a sketch of the car and the following day
the police arrested a plate of spaghetti and a
cake tin.

Fat Sam

A friend of mine had a cousin called Sam, a fat fellow who owned a disco in San Francisco. My friend Ivor went to visit him and he drove to 'Frisco in a rented hearse. He had a great time and then found that he'd lost the hearse. It wasn't until three days later he remembered where he'd left it and he sang, 'Ivor left my hearse in Fat Sam's disco ...'

She was the flabbiest stripper I've ever seen. When she ran off the stage she started her own applause.

A duck goes into a chemist's shop. 'A tube of lipsol, please.' The chemist said, 'Certainly. That'll be 50 pence.' 'Just put it on my bill.'

Man: 'Why are your hands so filthy?'
Barber: 'Nobody's asked for a shampoo yet.'

✻

I danced the polka with a typical German fraulein. She was the spitting image of Goering. The band played all the old German songs like 'Annie Get Your Luger' and a wartime song about paratroops from the Rhine Valley invading the town of Minehead. You might know it, it was called 'Rhine Troops are Falling on Minehead.'

✻

I was changing a tyre on my car the other day and a fellow pulled up and opened my bonnet. I said, 'What the hell do you think you're doing?'
He said, 'If you're having the wheels, I'm having the battery.'

✻

NEIGHBOURS

I HAVE A TERRIBLE GARDEN — I HAVE
TO HAVE A GREENHOUSE TO GROW
WEEDS — THE GROUND'S SO HARD I
PLANT SEEDS WITH A RAWLPLUG.
THE GRASS ON THE FRONT LAWNS SO
TALL EVERYTIME A FROG JUMPS THE
VET TREATS IT FOR A HERNIA.
MY WIFE CAME HOME THE OTHER NIGHT
IN A SAVAGE TEMPER SHE'D JUST BEEN
BEATEN IN A SNOOKER HANDICAP AND
SHE STARTED HITTING ME WITH A DRAIN
AND SMASHING OUR POT DOGS ON THE
MANTLEPIECE WITH HER CROSS BOW
GET GRASS CUT SHE SNARLED — HAVENT
GOT A LAWN MOWER — BORROW JONES
ACROSS THE ROAD — FULL GAG.

—— YOU KNOW YOUR ?
LAWN MOWER

—— WELL STICK IT

Judge: 'Is this the first time you've been up
before me?'
Prisoner: 'I don't know – what time do you
normally get up?'

Man in café: 'I want my toast burnt and the
egg running all over the plate.'
Waiter: 'We wouldn't serve anything like that.'
Man: 'Well, you did yesterday.'

Two flies on a bald head. One says to the
other, 'I remember when this was a footpath.'

My lad chewed and swallowed a dictionary.
We gave him Epsom salts – but we can't get a
word out of him.

What a girl – I first met her when she was
siphoning petrol out of a lawnmower.

The way prices are rising, the good old days
are last week.

My watch fell on the floor.
It wasn't broken, it fell on its hands.

My room is near the railway station. Every
time a train goes by it shakes so bad the
bedbugs use gliders.

Don't know where they got the steak from
but I was halfway through it when someone
shouted 'whoa!', and I damn near choked.

He died of drink – we cremated him and it
took eight weeks to put the fire out.

I crossed a parrot with a hen – got an egg
that tells you when it's done.

I saw an old woman carrying a basket of
fish. I said, 'Skate?'
She said, 'It takes me all my time to walk.'

A tramp is in court for stealing an overcoat.
Judge: 'My man, you're incorrigible! Three years ago you were up before me for stealing an overcoat and here you are again. What have you to say?'
Tramp: 'How long do you think overcoats last?!'

A man is pushing a piano on a cart.
Neighbour: 'Are you taking it back?'
Man: 'No, I'm going for my first lesson.'

A Scotsman returned from America after ten years. His two brothers met him, both with beards down to their knees. The returning Scotsman was annoyed. 'You both look a mess! My own brothers and ye meet me without having a shave!'
'It's your fault – when ye left ye took the razor!'

'Do you believe in free speech?'
'Yes. Can I use your phone?'

I won a trip to China. I'm there now trying
to win a trip back.

In the recent honours list there were six
shoemakers given the OBE. The Queen
was surprised. I wasn't; this government's
making cobblers of everything.

He once ran a mile in a minute – his braces
were caught in an E-Type Jag.

His brain is so weak he wears crutches
behind his ears.

His brain is so weak he wears crutches
behind his ears.

*

Man is born, lives and when dead we bury
him and he becomes dust and fertilizes the
Earth. So be careful what you tread in, it
could be your uncle.

*

She was so mean she went to have her finger read.

*

'Your son is in a class by himself.'
'Is he clever?'
'No. He smells.'

COURAGE

THE GERMAN OFFENSIVE OF 1915 HAD SCATTERED THE

ALLIED FORCES BACK ACROSS THE ~~R~~ SOMME AND

MOST REGIMENTS HAD DECIDED TO RETREAT.

WITH ONE EXCEPTION THE THIRD AND RIPON

MOUNTED FOOT. WHO'S MOTTO WAS "JOYA PAXO" -

ROUGHLY TRANSLATED: "GET THEESEN STUFFED"

ALL THAT WAS LEFT OF THE REGIMENT WAS THE

COLONEL: SIR WELLINGTON DE BOOTE AND HIS

BATMAN URIAH EARNSHAW. THEY BOTH STOOD IN

A MUD FILLED TRENCH AND THE COLONEL SHOUTED

DEFIANCE AT THE GERMANS THROUGH A MEGAPHONE.

"WE'LL NEVER SURRENDER YOU ROTTEN BOSCHE.

DO YOUR DAMNDEST. THE GERMANS REPLIED WITH

AN ARTILLERY BARRAGE — (WHISTLE) DOWN CAME

A PILE OF BEER BOTTLES AND SHREDDED WOODBINES

— (AND) EARNSHAW WHAT HAVE THEY HIT — THE

MOBILE NAAFI SIR — WE'LL NEVER GIVE IN

SHOUTED THE COLONEL THRU HIS MEGAPHONE — ANOTHER

SHELL — SHOWER OF UNDERPANTS — THEY'VE HIT THE

MOBILE LAUNDRY SIR WE'LL NEVER GIVE IN EARNSHAW.

WAR'S A FILTHY BUSINESS.

A fellow went to the doctor's. 'I've broken
my neck,' he said.

＊

'Keep your chin up,' the doctor replied.
A fellow went to a doctor and sneezed.
The doctor asked, 'Have you flu?'
'No, I came on the bus.'

＊

I think I'm a pair of curtains.
Well, pull yourself together.

＊

Heroism

Out of the Second World War came many stories of
valour and heroism. From Dunkirk to Normandy
the spirit of Britain was a burning torch that flamed
steadfast in the face of the jackbooted tyranny.

One story that has never been told outside the War Office sums up for all time the stoicism of our island race. It concerns flying officer Everett Lavender Gumboil, who used to be a ballet dancer in Runcorn.

One morning in 1943, he was flying one of ten Spitfires, and was going over to Germany on a leaflet raid. All the planes returned safely except for Everett's. All night they waited, but no sign of him. The mess was quiet; the commanding officer said hoarsely, 'He may have been a bit of a fruit, but a good type was old Everett.'

A fortnight went by and into view came Everett's Spitfire. Everybody rushed out to him, he got out and said, 'Oh what a fortnight I've had! The bullets, the noise!'

His commanding officer said, 'Where the hell have you been? The others dropped their leaflets and got back the same day!'

Everett replied, 'Did you say drop the leaflets? I've been shoving them through letter boxes!'

❉

I know a man who had injections for
smallpox, chicken pox and measles.
He died by leaking to death.

A man on a waterbed was set on fire and got poached to death.

A man divorced his wife because he'd heard divorcees were more passionate.

I think I'm going insane, doctor.
Yes, maddening, isn't it?

Why did you shoot your husband with a bow and arrow?
I didn't want to wake the kids!

The garage towed me two miles.
But I got my money's worth, I kept my
brakes on all the time.

He's the only man I know with a varicose
brain.

He went to a mind reader – and only got
charged half price.

He had a brain operation it cost £20 – and
that included £16 search fees.

A new dawn

The last thermo-nuclear bomb had been dropped. And all that remained of twentieth-century civilization was a grotesque forest of tangled steel and smouldering ruins, the choking radioactive clouds chivvied by a furnace. Hot winds roamed like predators over a lifeless planet and the silence was as profound as absolute zero.

In the cellar of a greengrocer's shop in Barnsley two scorched monkeys were sat eating fruit. One turned to the other, peeled an apple, and said, 'Here we go again, Eve.'

❋

The train was so crowded I got on reading a book called *The Grapes of Wrath* – I was so crushed I got off with a pint of wine.

Our climate gets worse. One day it's warm,
one day it's cold.
You never know what clothes to pawn.

The traffic on the roads gets even worse. I
saw a car in a traffic jam the other day with
'Just Married' on the boot and three kids in
the back.

You can't trust anybody. I went for a meal in
a café. When I got up to leave someone had
pinched my overcoat.

I said to the waiter, 'Somebody's took my
overcoat.'

The waiter said, 'I know.'

I said, 'Well, what did he look like?'

He said, 'Awful, the sleeves were too short.'

Hotels/Sportsmen

I made a pilgrimage recently to a site in Yorkshire where they're building a sewage works. As I watched the workmen scurrying like ants in the heaped clay, tears coursed down my cheeks because, only ten years ago, on that site stood one of the finest hotels in the world – The Ritz Waldorf Imperial, Otley.

I started work there as a wine chiller and rose to be under-manager of the third floor linen cupboards and brine bath.

One night I was sat in my office siphoning petrol from a lawnmower, when in came a porter called Horace Cakepole. He asked, 'Who's staying in room 94?' I said, 'The famous Olympic underwater swimmer, Pierre Cork. Why? What's wrong?'

He said, 'He's lying at the bottom of the swimming pool in the deep end, and I reckon he's a show off.'

'Why?' I asked

'Because he's been down there a month.'

The plane travels so fast you can eat a
pickled onion in London and belch in
Moscow.

He bought that suit by accident – it fits like a bandage.

❁

Man: 'I'd like some rat poison.'
Chemist: 'I haven't got any but why don't you try boots?'
Man: 'I want to poison 'em, not kick 'em to death.'

❁

He's a great doctor. He made an invigorating pill – cascara coated – he gave one to his eighty-seven-year-old grandfather who'd been bedridden sixty-five years – took one pill, couldn't stay in bed a minute.

❁

'Doctor, tell me, is it serious?'
'No, but don't bother buying any new suits.'

I said to the doctor, 'Will you sign me off?'
He said, 'That's impossible sir – you're
already a write-off.'

❀

We buried Aunt Cissie – had an awful letter
from the burial company – if we don't pay
the last instalment, up she comes.

❀

What's the world coming to? Every time
you open the newspapers it's Sex! Violence!
Robbery! And that's only the sports results.

❀

'I'll give you 40 pills in a box.'
'Thanks, its hopeless trying to roll 'em home.'

❀

'Does your nose burn?'
'Yes, if I set fire to it.'

❁

I love the women in Spain. Met a lovely girl
there – Carmen Cohen – she didn't know if
she was Carmen or Cohen.

❁

Oh, the women in France! Kim Novak,
Bridget Bardot, Gladys Maggs – that's the
one I went out with. She was so thin she had
latticework for varicose veins.

❁

'You run like Matthews.'
'Who? Stanley?'
'No, Jessie.'

What a quack

I'm not very keen on our local doctor, because quite frankly he's a bigger quack than Mother Goose. He's so old-fashioned he lances a boil on horseback and when he operates he doesn't use any anaesthetic, he makes you bite on a bullet. He'll have to retire soon as he's running out of leeches.

I saw him the other day. He said, 'Why don't you come and see me? I'm still practising.' I said, 'In that case, I'll come back when you're perfect.'

My neighbour old Cissie Ackroyd went to see him about her ninety-nine-year-old brother. She said he couldn't come himself as he's ill.

The doctor said, 'Illness stems from the subconscious – he only *thinks* he's ill. Tell him that, make him repeat it every day.' The following week the doctor called to see her. 'How's your brother now?'

'Oh, he's worse, doctor. He thinks he's dead!'

❧

Emmerdale Farm ... a sort of *Dynasty*
with dung.

Our house was so...

... damp, they didn't pull it down, they torpedoed it.

...damp, the gas meter was full of octopus droppings.

Our dining room was so damp we don't have a serving hatch, we have lock gates.

We got married in the backyard so the hens could peck the rice.

I discovered the wife's got asthma.
Thank God – I thought she was hissing at me.

Meanness

Sandy MacPuddle was close to death. He lay on his wooden bed with the sound of the sea booming around his Hebridean cottage. His wife was out swimming under the bridges and had left instructions to Sandy that if he felt himself slipping away, would he blow the candle out and order one egg for breakfast. Sandy wasn't looking at anything so he took his glasses off to save the lenses, and unlocked his purse so he could oil the turnstile in it.

The following night he was halfway in the arms of the Grim Reaper and all his family were gathered around.

His brother said, 'We'll make do with two cars – one for Sandy and one for the twelve of us.'

Sandy's wife said, 'One car will be enough; we can strap

Sandy on the luggage rack – that way we'll save an awful lot of money.'

An uncle in the corner said, 'Suppose we put wheels and a sail on the coffin and pray for a wind to carry him to the cemetery?'

At which point Sandy sat up and said, 'Pass me my trousers and I'll walk to the bloody cemetery!'

❀

Cowboys

My grandpappy was an old Indian fighter. That's what he married – an old Indian. In the Battle of Sioux River he had 100 arrows in his back and lived to tell the tale then died of woodworm.

I said, 'Those Indians, pappy, were they blackfoot?'

He said, 'I'm not sure, but their vests were filthy.'

I said, 'When you were on the plain, did you see any bison?'

'No, I had a wash in a bucket.'

My horse was on a coat hanger – it's a mustang. As I rode into Tombstone I fell over it and broke my collarbone. I was surrounded by redskins – I'd fallen on a tomato stall. A bald Indian came up so I sold him a hot poultice to keep in his wigwam – he said, 'Come to tepee.' I said, 'Thank you, I'm bursting.'

His wife was so fat she was the last squaw to break a camel's back.

Count Dracula

Perhaps the most horrific story ever told is the blood-curdling tale of Count Dracula. The first do-it-yourself blood bank. What isn't widely known is that he was engaged to a woman in Cleethorpes. She was a chef in a rissole bakery and at weekends played the accordion for Asian Morris dancers.

One blustery night in November, her drawers blew off the line and finished up in the local cemetery. As she was picking them up off a grave a hand came up and got its fingers caught in the gusset. She hit the hand with a burial urn and shouted, 'Get off you randy corpse!' Just then the earth parted and revealed Count Dracula.

'Good evening,' he said. 'I'm from Gravesend.'

'Oh, by your accent, I thought you were from Bury.'

He came closer and his fangs sank into her neck, and it was love at first bite. 'I'll never forget your teeth,' she said. 'Fangs for the memory.'

They went on courting for six months and spent their time in pubs with Dracula biting her neck in the vault. One day she was lying in bed white as a sheet and her mother said, 'I haven't seen you in the pub lately wit' fella wit' cloak and big teeth.'

She said, 'Nay, I've finished with him.'

'Why, lass?'

'Cos I'm fed up with being stuck for the drinks.'

Two years ago I went to Scotland and taught the hornpipe to strike pickets. During the exploding trouser riots I met Hamish Macquirtle. He was a son of the soil, his father was son of the soil and his grandfather was a son of the soil – in fact, they were the dirtiest family in Scotland.

He was engaged to a caber tossing dwarf called Winnie, who worked in a chamber pot factory. One night while playing squash in a pub vault, a cockney whispered in her ear, and she went straight to Hamish. 'Hamish,' she said, 'That man from Battersea has just offered me £5 if I'll make love to him all night.'

Hamish picked the cockney up and gave him a good hiding. When he'd finished, the cockney said, 'What did you do that for?'

Hamish said, 'That'll teach you to bring your London prices up here.'

✻

I
WOULDN'T
SAY. . .

I wouldn't say they were posh but the toilet
coughed before it flushed.

I wouldn't say they were posh but the mice made
trap reservations.

I wouldn't say the food was bad but Fanny
Craddock was picketing the oven.

I wouldn't say our kitchen smells, but sometimes
we leave the gas on to clear the air.

I wouldn't say the show was lousy but it was such
a cheap version of *South Pacific* it was called *South
Pathetic.*

I wouldn't say he drinks to excess but if he beats
you to the bar, you've had it.

I wouldn't say she was fat but the WeightWatchers wore blinkers.

I wouldn't say she was fat but when she went for a dress fitting the assistants worked in shifts.

I wouldn't say she was fat but when she wants a new dress she goes to a quantity surveyor.

I wouldn't say she's immature but she thinks Postman's Knock is a game of skill … Mind you, the way I play it, it is!

I wouldn't say she was fat but she doesn't wear corsets, she uses bailing wire.

I wouldn't say she was fat but she had so many chins she uses a bookmark to find her mouth.

I wouldn't say the house was damp but the kids went to bed with a periscope.

I wouldn't say the house was damp but the woodworm breathed through straws.

I wouldn't say the house was damp but the goldfish climbed out of the bowl to breath.

I wouldn't say the house was damp but we didn't go into the cellar for coal unless we wore shark repellent.

I wouldn't say the wife talks too much, but all the parrot can say is, 'But … But … But …'

I wouldn't say the rooms were small but we used a folding toothbrush in the bathroom.

I wouldn't say the room was small but you had to buy bananas ready peeled.

I wouldn't say she was skinny but her legs were so bony her knees made a fist.

I wouldn't say the room was small but the woodworm were round-shouldered.

I wouldn't say the room was small but when I talked to myself one of us had to step outside to reply.

I wouldn't say the room was small but the toaster lay on its side.

I wouldn't say the room was small but you had to
soak your dentures in shifts.

I wouldn't say my daughter's promiscuous but
when they had a sex education lesson at school
she embarrassed the teacher.

I wouldn't say the plane was old but they didn't
say, 'Fasten your seatbelts', they shouted, 'Buckle
your breastplates.'

I wouldn't say she was thin, but I've seen more
meat on a British Rail sandwich.

I wouldn't say she's fast but if you're planning an
orgy, she's the girl to organize it.

I wouldn't say the plane was old but we were
hijacked by the Wright Brothers.

I wouldn't say she was ugly but her face was lifted
so often they had to lower her body.

I wouldn't say he's got a big mouth but he can eat a
banana in one – sideways.

I wouldn't say she was ugly but the milkman flirts
with me.

I wouldn't say she was ugly but she went for a
swim in Loch Ness and the monster got out and
picketed the lake.

I SAID TO THE WIFE . . .

It's a funny thing how you meet the woman that you marry. I met the wife in a tunnel of love. She was digging it.

❀

My wife said, 'You remind me of the sea.'
I said, 'You mean restless, wild and passionate?'
'No, you make me sick.'

❀

Wife: 'I want a man who can kiss me like Rock Hudson, hold me like Marlon Brando and make my blood boil like Kirk Douglas.'
I said: 'I can bite you like Lassie.'

❀

My wife's so ignorant. We saw a pile of milk bottles. She said, 'Look! A cow's nest.'

Reasonable

I once fell in love with a lady contortionist. She used to bend over backwards and pick up a handkerchief with her teeth. Then for an encore she used to pick up her teeth. What a figure – you couldn't tell if she had bare legs or stockings lined with grapefruit. I asked her one night if she was free. She said no but she'd be reasonable. I called her Daisy because she grew wild on the grass. I'm not saying she was fat but she used to model circus tents. And what a face! She once sucked on a lemon and the lemon pulled a face. She was so ugly she got a job advertising iodine. She had some ways – she used to go to bed with a ruler to see how long she'd slept.

When you dance with someone you care for, to some their eyes grow misty with emotion; others, their throats become dry; and some people find their hearts beat faster. When I first danced with the wife I got a tingling sensation in my leg – she was scratching me with her bike clips.

> SONG PARODIES
>
> 1 "MAMMY MAMMY – I'D WALK A MILLION MILES
>   IF IT WASN'T FOR PILES MY MAMMY"
>
> ————————.—————————
>
> 2 "MY AUNTIE FANNY BY MISTAKE PUT SENNA PODS IN A CURRANT CAKE
>   AND THE ONLY THING THAT SHE COULD DO WAS – SLIP TO
>   THE LOO MY DARLIN"
>
> ————————.—————————
>
> 3 "HOW MANY BEANS WILL YOU FIND IN A TIN – HOW MANY BEANS
>   WILL THERE BE? THE ANSWER MY FRIEND IS BLOWING IN THE
>   WIND"

I went to my wife's father, 'I'd 'er 'er.'

'Certainly you can have her, son, with pleasure.'

'Have who?'

'My daughter's hand in marriage, of course!'

'No, you don't understand – I want to borrow a fiver off you.'

'Not likely – I hardly know you!'

I took her for better or for worse. But she turned out worse than I took her for.

Eating out

I took the wife out the other night to a restaurant. The waitress came over, picking her nose. I said, 'Have you got eczema?'

She said, 'Only what you see on the menu.'

We ordered crab. When it came the wife said, 'It stinks.'

The waiter said it was fresh from the sea this morning.

The wife said, 'Well it must have trod in something on the way out.'

She's no idea, my wife. She once sent a plate of scampi back because she said it smelt fishy – and her table manners are atrocious. I took her on a cruise last year and when she drank her soup the captain stood up and shouted, 'Abandon ship!'

Apart from the wife grumbling about the crab, I enjoyed my night out, until I got the bill. I said to the waiter, 'This is far too much for what we've had.'

He said, 'I assure you it's the correct amount. I have the chits.'

I said, 'What the bloody hell do you think I've got?'

After the meal I said to the waiter, 'What about the tip?'

He said, 'Leave it, I'll clean the mess up when you've gone.'

My wife's not lost her looks … she's just as ugly as the day I married her.

✻

The neighbours think I'm a ventriloquist. When I open my mouth she speaks.

She had a blemish between her ears – a head.

✻

My wife's so thin, I've seen more fat on a cold chip.

✻

She has a big lower lip – but you didn't notice it because her top lip covered it.

My wife's so ugly – when she was a child she used to 'play penny or a kiss'. At the age of eighteen she bought a car.

✻

What a cook

I bought her a pressure cooker. God knows what she did with it but she's the first woman I know to put a turnip in orbit. She came lumbering into our room the other night reeking of gin and her nightdress was covered in snuff stains. I could tell she was upset because her eye patch wasn't on properly and her duelling scar was livid.

She shook my shoulder with a hand the size of a dinner gong and whispered, 'There's a prowler downstairs.'

I asked, 'What's he doing?'

She said, 'He's sat in the kitchen eating my homemade rissoles.'

So I got back into bed.

She said, 'Aren't you going to phone for the police?'

'Why bother?' I replied. 'I'll go down in the morning and bury him.'

I was lying in bed the other morning playing a lament on my euphonium when the wife, who was prising her teeth out of an apple, looked at me and said softly, 'Joey.' She calls me Joey because she always wanted a budgie.

She said, 'I'm homesick.'

I said, 'But, precious one, this is your home.' She said, 'I know, and I'm sick of it.'

I'm not saying the wife's fat, but she puts her knickers on with a tyre lever.

I live like a king.
When I go home I get crowned.

73

The wife bought a chicken last week. It was
so old its beak was crowned and capped.

✽

She was so ignorant, she thought a
millimetre was a Spanish earwig.

✽

She was only a sewage worker's daughter but
she was nothing to be sniffed at. She was stood
putting snuff up her nose with the end of a snooker
cue. She had a donkey under her arm – she just had
it for kicks.

I said, 'Can I hire that donkey?'

She said, 'Yes there's a screw under its saddle.'

She was a funny looking woman, she had so
many chins the bottom one was soled and heeled.

✽

Marriage is an institution and that's where a
couple finish up.

I wouldn't say...

... the walls in our house are thin but if I hang a picture up in the lounge, the nail pierces the next-door neighbour's ear.

... the room was small but the fleas on the dog's back didn't jump for fear of concussion.

Two can live as cheaply as one – providing she's got lockjaw.

My wife is a suicide blonde – dyed by her own hand.

She's the only woman I know with
Technicolor dandruff.

*

When we met time stood still – the clock stopped.

*

She had her face lifted – but they'd tightened
the skin so much when she raised her
eyebrows she hitched her knickers up.

*

She's just like her mother. Ah, I can see her now,
with that funny hat on, huddled over a steaming
cauldron. And then flying out the window on her
broomstick.

HoliDAYS

I DON'T SUPPOSE YOU'VE EVER HEARD OF MY BROTHER-IN-LAW HIS NAME IS GILBERT KNUCKLE AND HE'S MARRIED TO THE WIFE'S ELDEST SISTER PRUNELLA - WE CALL HER PRUNE FOR SHORT BECAUSE SHE'S ALWAYS ON THE MOVE - SHE WAS MISS SIENNA POD 1956 - A REAL GO GO GIRL. THEY LIVE MILES FROM ANYWHERE IN A RECONDITIONED RECTORY AND THEY HAVE A PET GOOSE CALLED MAURICE - LAST YEAR GILBERT WON FIRST PRIZE IN A BARN DANCE SPOT WALTZ WHICH WAS A YEAR'S SUPPLY OF LETTUCE AND A WEEK'S HOLIDAY IN SHANGHAI. FIRST NIGHT THEY WERE THERE THEY SAT DOWN IN A CAFE AND ORDERED A MEAL ~~CHICKEN~~ - PRUNELLA SAID CHICKEN PLEASE THE WAITER SAID CHICKEN ALSO

A wife was determined to cure her husband's drinking. He staggered into bed one night, and she came in with a sheet over her head carrying a torch. He sat up and screamed, 'Who's that?'

'The devil,' said his wife.

They shook hands. 'Oh, I married your sister.'

My wife is so ignorant. She has no idea of anything – especially music. She thought Bizet's Carmen was a Spanish bus driver.

Clergymen

Our local vicar came to see us the other day to say goodbye before he left for his new parish.

The wife said, 'We'll be sorry to see you go, vicar. We didn't know what sin was until you came.'

Personally, I never liked him. He'd no sense of humour – he had to make an appointment to see a joke. And his sermons were so boring people used to put pep pills in the collection plate.

One Sunday he was worse than ever. The church bell had muffled its clapper. He looked at his congregation and thundered, 'You dismal sinners! Look at you all, asleep, except for that poor man you have the audacity to call the Village Idiot!'

The Village Idiot stood up and shouted, 'Aye, and if I wasn't so bloody daft I'd be asleep with 'em!'

WHEN I WAS A LAD . . .

A hard drinker

My mother, bless her, was musically minded. As a child, I used to climb on her knee and whisper, 'Mummy, Mummy, sing me lullaby do.'

And she'd say, 'Certainly, my little angel, my wee bundle of happiness. Hold me beer while I fetch me banjo.'

Mother wasn't a hard drinker – she found it easy. She was in hospital for a week and Guinness shares dropped. We had so many empty beer bottles in the backyard it put £300 on the price of the house.

The vicar said to her once, 'You wicked woman. Every time I see you you've got a bottle in your hand.'

Mother said, 'Well, I can't keep it in my mouth all day.'

What a woman. She crawled home from so many pubs we had her fitted out with crab feelers.

I think my father used to collect old musical instruments – at least the police used to call round once a week and ask him where he'd put the loot. He's been in jail so often when he did finally go straight the prison missed him so much they asked him to go back part-time.

When I was a child, I had wax in my ears.
Dad didn't take me to the doctor, he used me
as a night light.

I'm not saying I was an ugly baby, but as I
was being born the midwife took one look
at me and shouted to my mother, 'For God's
sake, bear up!'

Sporting feats

My granddad was a boxer and my grandmother was
a cocker spaniel. I was a boxer too but I wasn't very
good. I was known as 'Wash Day' because I was
always hanging over the ropes. I was carried out of
the ring so often I had handles sewn on my shorts.
In my first fight the referee said to my opponent,
'You'll be disqualified if you hit him below the belt,'
so I wore turtle-necked shorts.

What a fight that was – I was so far behind on

points I had to knock the other fellow out to get a draw.

I was a superstitious boxer – I wouldn't fight without a horseshoe in my glove. In my last fight I got knocked out so cold they picked me up with ice tongs.

Then I became a footballer. I ran like Best – not George ... Edna. I tried weightlifting. I once press lifted 900lbs in a competition and on winning it added yet another wonderful double hernia to my record.

My grandfather played the trombone in bed. It upset gran – chipped paint off her guitar.

My father was a small man. In fact he suffered from athlete's foot on his chin.

Mother was so tiny she had castors on
her earrings.

❀

Dad wanted me to call me Simon – because
I was beginning to look so simple.

❀

We had a great big piano – a family could
have lived in it – then they'd all have their
own key.

❀

I had a very strict upbringing. I wasn't
allowed in the house till I was eight.

I'm not saying my mother didn't like me but she kept looking for loopholes in my birth certificate.

❀

My parents did a double act – it resulted in a failure – me.

❀

A hard life...

The main ingredient in the crucible of society is the family. Everyone's got a family tree – mine's a weeping willow. My mother used to look at me and say, 'I don't know what to make of him.'

And my father used to say, 'Have you thought of a rug?'

Dad didn't like me, in fact the night I was kidnapped by gypsies, it was Father who drove the caravan for them. We lived in a poor district. We were living up to the Joneses next door – and they were under the care of Oxfam. Things were so bad we used to go out and rob tramps.

It was a broken home. Everything we used we broke. The only thing in good condition was the bath. We weren't a very clean family. The safest place to keep money was under the soap. I was a mess – I had understains on my understains.

My family were unusual people. My grandmother was raised for the law. At least I once heard the neighbours say she was brought up for soliciting. My grandfather was an athlete – a famous shot putter. He was picked for the Olympics until they saw where he was putting it. He was a fine-looking man – he got a part in the film *The Hunchback of Notre Dame* but got fired because he kept slipping down off Charles Laughton's shoulder.

My uncle was an actor. He once played a
supporting role in a jungle picture – he
was Tarzan's truss. He enjoyed it – told
everybody he'd had a ball.

Funny how you get into this business, though I suppose the stage was in my blood. My great grandmother was a gaiety girl in London – men drank champagne from her slipper and blew kisses in her ear. She died at the age of ninety-eight, deaf and with damp feet.

❋

My father was a big drinker – my birth certificate was printed on a cork.

❋

Mother didn't want me – she got my bath ready one night and when I put my duck in the water, it melted.

❋

Mother ran the house like clockwork – everything we had was on tick.

Red Indian

When I was a small boy of seven I wandered away from a school nature ramble and found myself lost and alone on a bleak moor that was swept by a spiteful wind. Cuffed and buffeted by its anger I sought refuge under a frowning crag and when the wind finally died away to a whimper I crept out and, looking up, I saw an old Red Indian squatting on top of the rock, his coppery profile thrown like a rare coin against the blue-dipped sky. His voice when he spoke was like somebody drawing a rake across dried leaves.

He said, 'Me Red Cloud. Me know all. Remember everything.'

Childishly, in my frightened state, I shouted, 'What did you have for breakfast thirty years ago?'

He smiled, puckered his razor-thin lips and whispered, 'Egg.'

The years scampered away but never once did I forget the old wise man. And last Wednesday, mentally worn and physically beaten by the world's demands, I drove to that bleak moor and stumbled across to the rock where I knew he would be – and he was – just as I remembered him, hunched in his blanket as still as the crag he sat on. In my eagerness to greet him I raised my hand and shouted, 'How.'

He said, 'Fried.'

My brother did 100 yards in ten seconds –
he fell down a lift shaft.

We were so poor our mouse left us and went
to live with the church mice.

We were so poor that when dad was in prison
on bread and water he put six stone on.

We were so poor, after the flag seller had
called we had to fire a distress rocket.

Christmas

The best we could manage was five-a-side to a cracker, and the Christmas dinner was always the same – Scotch pheasant – it was black pudding with a feather stuck in it.

I remember with embarrassment how my father's feet were so dirty that every time he hung his stocking up the tree died. I can only recall being given one Christmas box, it was called a do-it-yourself electric train set – turned out to be a roll of fuse wire and a platform ticket …

Mind you, that Christmas period started out on the wrong foot. The local butcher charged the wife £10.50 for a turkey. I don't know how long he'd had it in stock, but when I plucked it I found it had an appendix scar. But what really made me mad was when I lifted up its wing I saw somebody had written 'Kilroy was here'. Actually it didn't taste too bad. I complimented the wife. 'What did you stuff it with?' I asked.

She said, 'I didn't have to bother, sweetheart, it was already full.'

She has no idea … she made a Christmas pudding and the only tender part of it was the threepenny bit inside. Then, to crown it all the wife's family descended on us. They went at the food like a shoal of piranha fish. I've never seen table manners like theirs, they made the chimps tea party look like morning coffee with Godfrey Winn.

The wife's mother got plastered and sang the songs she learned as a stormtrooper. I didn't say anything. It's hard to describe what she's like but last August she stood on the cliffs at Southend in a bikini and all you could see was illegal immigrants diving in screaming and swimming for home.

We hadn't a telly. We used to sit and watch
the fire go out. Then we'd go and order
another shovelful of coal.

There's a very strong military strain in my family. My great-great grandfather fought in the Boer War. He was a veteran of many campaigns – never decorated, but if his behaviour is any guide, frequently plastered.

But music was my yearning. As a boy I used
to get carried away playing the piano –
mostly by the neighbours.

My father bred and transported bulls for
fighting.
He was the biggest bull shipper in the
country.

Friendship

I've always been a lonely person; nobody ever
wanted me. When I was a baby I was left on so
many doorsteps I thought daddy was a milk bottle.
Mummy never used talcum powder on me – I
really roughed it. I had nappy rash on my nappy
rash. Once she used self-raising flour on me and I
broke out in Jaffa Cakes. When I grew up the only
friend I had was a grapefruit – but it was vicious if
you bit it as it went for the eyes.

One day I was in an antique shop looking for a

SITUATION SCRIPT
"BUYING A HOUSE."

"IT'S A NICE HOUSE — ONLY 1350 — THAT WAS
THE YEAR IT WAS BUILT. WE'RE BUSY BUYING
THINGS FOR IT, LITTLE THINGS FOR OUR
COMFORT — A BACK-DOOR; WINDOW FRAMES.
ONLY TROUBLE IS THE PEOPLE NEXT DOOR.
3 AM THIS MORNING BANGING ON THE WALLS
AND SCREAMING — GOOD JOB I WASN'T
TRYING TO GET TO SLEEP; I WAS PLAYING
MY DRUMS AT THE TIME. WHEN WE STARTED
LOOKING FOR A HOUSE OUR BABY WAS
10 MONTHS OLD — HE'S 39 NOW.

copy of Barry Cryer's *Topical Gags*. They hadn't got one; the archaeologists were still digging for them in Greece.

Lonely, I walked on past a pet shop and saw a beautiful budgie in a golden cage. The pet shop owner said it talked like W.C. Fields, sang like Vic Damone and spoke Shakespeare like John Gielgud. I took it home but it never spoke nor sang. I bought it a silver bell, a perch, a gilt-edged mirror and it still didn't sing or speak. Lying on the floor one day, it croaked, 'You forgot the bloody bird seed.'

Mother had most of the things that men
desire – muscles and a moustache.

A billy goat used to look after me as a baby –
we couldn't afford a nanny.

Dad was called Ben, ma was called Anna –
according to that I'm a benanna.

My father wanted me to be an athlete. He
threw me in the canal, which is hard for boy of
six. The worst part was getting out of the sack.

My grandfather made money out of the slave
trade – he sold my grandmother.

Grandad

Tonight is a special night for my family. It marks
the anniversary of my great grandfather, who
gave Alaska its first piece of folklore. In 1889 he
was prospecting for gold in the Mackenzie river and
he fell in love with an Eskimo maiden who used to
blow kisses to him across the icy stretch of water.
He couldn't get across to her – the water was too
treacherous – and for ten years they called out their
love to each other from opposite banks. In 1909 he
could stand it no longer. He jumped into the icy water
to reach her and within ten minutes he was frozen to
death. The Eskimos still tell of the legend of their love
and the water is still called after him – Lake Twit.

When I was a lad my teeth stuck out so
much Mother rented me out as a till.

PROPOSED SCRIPT

I'VE HAD SOME BAD NEWS ABOUT THE WIFE'S WEALTHY
UNCLE WHO'S ILL IN HOSPITAL — HE'S RECOVERING — WENT
TO SEE HIM LAST WEEK I SAID IS THERE ANYTHING I
CAN DO FOR YOU — HE SAID ONLY ONE — TAKE YOUR
FOOT OFF THE OXYGEN TUBE. —

❋

My father was in the horse artillery, but the
feedbag kept falling off his ears.

❋

Dad took me for boxing lessons.
The instructor said, 'He fights like the Great
Wilde!'
I said, 'You mean Jimmy Wilde?'
He said, 'No, Oscar.'

❋

MY AUNT BOUGHT LUCKY CHARM MASCOT
—— AND THROTTLED HERSELF IN THE
MANGLE

—— . ——

MY NEIGHBOURS DON'T PEEP THRU'
CURTAINS —— THEY'VE GOT RADAR

—— . ——

BARBER'S SHOP SIGN: "DURING ALTERATIONS
CUSTOMERS WILL BE SHAVED AT THE
REAR

—— . ——

PICTURE SO OLD —— THE INDIANS ATTACKING
THE FORT WEREN'T KIDDING

—— . ——

MY WIFE SAID JUST THINK ONE
DAY I MAY BE OLD AND BAGGY
—— WHY WORRY ABOUT TOMORROW?

—— . ——

MICK JAGGER —— WEARS HIS PANTS OUT
FROM THE INSIDE

—— . ——

My father was a keen Trades Unionist.
He insisted on a tea break on his wedding
night.

Dear old dad

My father once stumbled over a crate of whiskey – and he went on stumbling for the next three months. His nose became so red he was banned from the coast because he was a hazard to shipping. He drank so heavily when he blew on a birthday cake he lit the candles. He was on the floor so often he got a job modelling lino. Mind you, he was good, he only kicked me down the stairs once a day and he gave mother half of everything he stole – then suddenly after listening to a long-playing record of Billy Graham – he reformed. We had to get the doctor to look at Father eventually. He diagnosed a severe attack of moth bites. My father said, 'Impossible. We've a wardrobe full of moths and I know them all by their first names.'

Gone fishin'

My godfather was a retired spittoon engraver from Doncaster and his wife was a six-foot ex-Nazi guard dog trainer. She used to hit him every night on the top of his head with a boxing glove. He was the only man I knew with cauliflower eyebrows and punch-drunk dandruff.

One day she won £1,000 in a karate stranglehold contest and went to America to visit her uncle in the Mafia. The following week he got a telegram from a university aquarium in Chicago. It read, 'Sorry to inform you that your wife was drowned yesterday. When her body was recovered a rare fish was found hanging off her foot. The American government has offered £10,000 for the fish – wire instructions.'

He wrote back, 'Accept offer and re-set the bait.'

My mother wanted me to be brought up at Eton.
My father said, 'He looks as if he's been eaten and
brought up.'

❀

One day a teacher said, 'Find me the Alps.'
I said, 'Can't you remember where you put
them?'

❀

I used to be a boxer.
I fought like Cooper – not Henry, Gladys.

❀

There were so many of us, Mother didn't
give us names, she had us branded.

THERE'S NO DOUBT ABOUT IT my LIFE'S GETTING BONE IDLE — SHE KNEW DAMN WELL I WAS COMING TO DO THE SHOW TONIGHT AND I STILL HAD TO SHOUT HER THREE TIMES TO COME UP AND DRESS ME.

"RED HEAD — NO HAIR — JUST A RED-HEAD" — LIKE A PEACH — YELLOW & FUZZY"

FAMILY MATTERS

I've had some bad news about the wife's wealthy uncle who's ill in hospital. He's recovering. I went to see him last week.

I said, 'Is there anything I can do for you?'

He said, 'Only one thing. Take your foot off the oxygen tube.'

❊

The wedding

Of all the horrors that society can inflict upon us in our brief lives, nothing chills my blood more than that time-honoured tradition – the wedding reception. It usually starts about half an hour after the wedding ceremony. It's held either in a hall the size of Wembley or a living room designed for midgets.

I went to one last week. The wife's eldest sister married a fellow who told us he was in the oil business. I found out after that he was a sardine packer. The wedding was held at three o'clock. I'm not saying the bride looked a mess but the vicar wore blinkers. To start with she's a funny shape, built like a jar of Bovril. She was wearing a wedding dress that fitted her like a glove – an oven glove. When she knelt at the altar, her corsets burst and we had to

LES DAWSON'S JOKE BOOK

hold her in place with guy ropes. The wife said her sister was pushing forty. Frankly, she looked as if she was dragging it.

Her husband was wearing a hired dress suit. I'm not saying he looked a mess but Moss Bros. was picketing the church.

I've never seen a fellow so small: every time he pulls his socks up he gets a wool rash on his ears. He knelt at the altar and you could tell his nose was running as there was a rainbow round his neck. The vicar looked at the bride, looked at the size of the groom and said, 'Do you take this woman or will you have her delivered?'

The reception was held in the mother-in-law's house. She'd obviously spent a bob or two on it – for a start there was smoked salmon on the table and nobody ill. We all had a glass of lukewarm sherry – it tasted awful. God knows who trod the grapes for it but he must have had athlete's foot. Everyone went for the food like runaway bullocks. I've never seen table manners like it – it made the chimps' tea party look like an evening out with the Galloping Gourmet.

The wife's mother sat glaring at the groom's family like a bucolic ferret. The father-in-law was sat holding her hand; if he'd let go she'd have killed him. Poor devil, he's frightened to death of her! It's been so long since he opened his mouth, his tonsils blink at the light. He's as bald as a badger – he has to sprinkle his pillow with sand to stop his head sliding off.

The wife's youngest sister was there too. She's so bandy she irons her drawers over a boomerang. And talk about thin, when she turns sideways with her tongue out she looks like a zip. She caught measles when she was a kid and there was only room for one spot.

The wife's brother was present, drunk as usual, but he was enjoying himself. I could see that from the way he was lay. I've never met anyone so bone-idle. He's the only man I know who gets a pension for bedsores. He used to be a bricklayer. Nobody knows how long he's been out of work, but the last wall he built was Hadrian's. He staggered over and asked me to lend him a fiver. I told him I'd only got £4 and he said, that's fine, you can owe me one.

The mother put a record on the radiogram and we started dancing. It didn't last long; you can't dance for long to 'The Laughing Policeman'.

Neither side of the family talked to the other; our side sat down on one side of the room and their lot sat down on the other. It looked like the start of a tag-wrestling match.

The bridegroom's father was a bit peculiar – he said he trained donkeys for 6p a lesson. I asked him, 'What do you do first with a wild donkey?' He said, 'Hit it over the head with a 9 foot 6 inch thick plank.'

'What for?' I asked.

'That's lesson number one, first gets it's attention.'

I wouldn't say things were bad...

... but round our way the bank's only open for hold ups.

... but there's so much squalor in our town that the Lord Mayor suggested we make fungus our national flower.

He was strong.
Not looked it – smelt it.

He had so many bullets in him, they didn't give him a military funeral, they weighed him in.

The population explosion

Everybody keeps saying that there are too many people in the world. The trouble with the population explosion is that it's such fun lighting the fuse. More twins are being born than ever before because kids are scared coming into the world alone.

I knew a man called Alfred Knucklebottom who had a walrus farm in Skegness. His wife was a traffic warden who'd lost her lip in an avalanche. They'd been married ten years and had nine kids – they would have had ten but Alfred had been locked in a cupboard for a fortnight. A year later, after a coach trip to Cromer, his wife gave birth to two sets of quins. Alfred was coming out of the hospital when the vicar saw him. He said, 'Ah! I hear that the Lord has smiled on you again.'

Alf said, 'Smiled? He's had a bloody good laugh!'

I have a friend who's a lion tamer.
He used to be a teacher until he lost his
nerve …

It's a family affair

My little lad was saying his prayers last night. Halfway through them he shouted at the top of his voice, 'And please God send me a big red fire engine price £2 from Johnson's Toy Shop!'

I said, 'There's no need to shout, son. God isn't deaf.'

He said, 'I know, but Mother is.'

Children. Where would we be without them? It's a well-known fact that if your parents didn't have children neither will you.

Before our last kiddie was born I said to my 'daughter,' 'What would you like, a girl or a boy?'

She said, 'A lickle sister to play wiv and share my dollies wiv and play at house and fings …'

I said to my youngest lad, 'I suppose you'd like a little brother?'

He said, 'If it won't put our mam put of shape too much I'd like a donkey.'

Mind you, their inherent honesty sometimes embarrasses you. I took my little lad to see my wealthy uncle who's been ill. He said, 'Uncle, do me an impression of a frog.'

'What for?' said uncle.

He said, 'Every time I ask dad for money he keeps saying wait till your uncle croaks …'

The only decent thing we had in our house was cheap air-conditioning, until some fool killed the bat.

✹

They tell us parents we should love our kids. We should kiss them before they go to bed at night. But who's going to stay up until they've gone to bed?

✹

You don't get rougher

There's a small boy near me who comes from a very tough family – so tough there's a notice on their gate that reads 'Beware the Grandma'. He's a dirty little kid – the last time he had a bath his mother pulled out the plug and pushed the water down with a poker. He's never got a handkerchief and the only song he knows is 'Greensleeves'.

He's got a pet, a one-eyed mongrel dog with so many fleas that its tail is an overspill estate. He took it to the Crufts dog show last year. He sat outside and a girl came up with a golden retriever. The mongrel barked at it and the girl said, 'Take that disgusting creature away. My Labrador's just been awarded two firsts in its class, and a highly commended.'

The boy said, 'That's nothing, mine's had two fights, one bitch and he's highly delighted!'

❀

And they expect us to teach our kids the facts of life. I finally plucked up courage and told my son about the birds and the bees.

When I finished I said, 'Well, son, you heard what I told you. Now what do you say?"

He said, 'Not bad, Dad. You got most of it right.'

❀

I said to my doctor, 'Is it possible for a nine-year-old child to take out an appendix?
He said, 'No.'
I said to my son, 'See? Now put it back!'

❀

Never forget...

Old Hamish McQuirtle was a widower and he was in hospital recovering from a major operation. He'd been ill for over four months and his three sons hadn't brought him anything: no flowers or grapes, nothing at all. Finally he sent for his family and they all stood around his bed. There was his eldest son Albert – he was so mean he took long steps to make his shoes last longer. His next son, Dermot, was the same: a wealthy fish manure wholesaler from Perth, he once found a crutch and not wanting to waste it, he broke his wife's leg.

McQuirtle's youngest son, Rory, was just as mean – he'd once broke into a neighbour's house to gas himself.

Hamish looked at them: 'No grapes, no flowers, no papers, no tobacco, ah you mean lot.'

'Forgive us, dad, it was just forgetfulness.'

'Aye. I'll forgive you. We're all guilty of forgetfulness. For example, I forgot to marry your mother.'

'Father, do you mean we're all…?' they shouted.

Hamish said, 'Aye, and three bloody cheap ones at that!'

Our house was so...

...dirty the mice suffered from blackheads.

...cold we put the milk in the fridge to stop it freezing.

The windows were so dirty they took the enamel off the cleaner's bucket.

AND NOW, ALTHOUGH YOU HAVE NEVER DONE ME ANY HARM, I INSIST ON PLAYING THE PIANO FOR YOU, IF ONLY TO PROVE HOW VERSATILE A ROTTEN ACT CAN BE...

—.—

CRIME

THE NAME WIMBERRY SOCKROT IS NOW FORGOTTEN
BUT 30 YEARS AGO HE WAS FAMOUS AS THE
FIRST ENGLISHMAN TO ~~SIT~~ SIT ON TOP OF ~~ALICE FAYE~~
AND JUGGLE WITH A TON OF LOOSE SOOT. HE MADE A
~~FORTUNE~~ GIVING PYGMIES TAP DANCE LESSONS.
~~HE~~ HE INVESTED HIS MONEY IN A ~~
FLEA CIRCUS BUT BUSINESS WAS LOUSY AND
BEFORE LONG HE WAS SCRATCHING FOR A LIVING.
HE BECAME A MISERABLE SPECIMAN OF HUMANITY
AND FINISHED UP IN COURT ACCUSED OF STEALING
AN OVERCOAT FROM A BINGO HALL — THE JUDGE
SAID SOCKROT YOU SCOUNDREL TWO YEARS AGO
YOU WERE UP BEFORE ME FOR STEALING
AN OVERCOAT — WHAT ~~MADE~~ YOU ~~DO IT AGAIN~~
~~SAY~~? WIMBERRY STOOD IN THE DOCK IN HIS SMELLING
RAGS AND SAID HOW LONG YOU THINK
AN OVERCOAT LASTS?

LIMERICKS

There was a young man from Bombay
Who sailed off to China one day
He was strapped to the tiller
With a sex-starved gorilla
And China's a bloody long way.

Robin and his Merry Men
They frolic in the sun.
And if you ask, 'Who's Maid Marion?'
They answer, 'Everyone!'

There was an old chap quite absurd
Who thought he could fly like a bird
Watched by thousands of people
He leapt down from a steeple
He was buried on April the third.

There was an old farmer from Greece
Who did terrible things to his geese
But he went too far with a budgerigar
And the parrot phoned the police.

There was an old maid from Genoa
And I blush when I think what Iowa
Now she's gone to her rest
And it's all for the best
Otherwise I'd borrow Samoa.

I got up this morning when the sun didn't shine
I picked up my shovel and I walked to the mine
I loaded sixteen tons of number 9 coal
And the foreman said, 'You bloody fool, you're on
two till ten this week.'

Schubert had a horse called Sarah
He rode her in a big parade
And all the time that the band was playing
Schubert's Sarah neighed.

❀

When I was a young boy and drove my mother wild
I met a maiden in the wood and she said to me
  'Child,
I'm going to show you a new game, of its fun you'll
  soon evince'
I don't know what it was we played
But cricket's had it since.

❀

If Communists are equal
Perhaps it would be fun
To ask why Stalin had so much hair
And poor old Khrushchev none.

Oh how I miss my ma-in-law
Sometimes it has me scared
That I will go on missing her
Until I get my rifle repaired.

A leaf it fell upon my foot
And to move it I was unable
The leaf was made of solid oak
From Auntie Aggie's table.

A pious young lady called Pond
Of wearing black frilly garters was fond
She said one day, as she knelt down to pray
They're in memory of those gone Beyond.

There was an old barrow boy from Mill Hill
Who swallowed an atomic pill
They found his barrow way up in Harrow
And his nuts up a tree in Brazil.

There was a young Scotsman called Andy
Who went into a pub for a shandy
As he lifted his kilt
To wipe up what he'd spilt
The barmaid said, 'Blimey! That's handy.'

There was an old farmer called Burk
Who pulled up his cart with a jerk
His load of manure was quite insecure
And he was up to his neck in his work.

My dear wife swallowed a pocket watch
T'was only the other day ...
And now she's taking Epsom Salts
To pass the time away.

NO, REALLY, TAKE MY WIFE . . .

She told me it was her thirtieth birthday so I
put thirty candles on her cake – arranged in
the shape of a question mark.

※

I said to the wife, 'I wish you wouldn't smoke
in bed.'
She said, 'But a lot of women do.'
I said, 'Not bacon, they don't.'

※

They say time heals all wounds, but it caused
most of mine.
The wife hit me with an alarm clock.

※

We've been married ten years now – a
decade – and, believe me, she has decayed.

On the plane

If brains were elastic, my wife wouldn't have enough for a flea's truss. I asked her once what she thought of apartheid. She said, 'I'm not sure but I think the pill's safer.' She honestly thought the film *Ben Hur* was about a sex change Scotsman. God knows when she last read a newspaper but she still goes to sleep in an air raid shelter.

Last year I talked her into going to Madeira for our annual holiday. She didn't want to go because she didn't fancy eating cake for a fortnight. We went on a cheap excursion flight. The plane was an early jet – a bag of charcoal and an oven. The pilot had a word with us – you could tell he was the pilot because his cap was back to front and he had goggles on. He said, 'I'm sorry to say the wings have fallen off and the propellers' rotted.'

The wife turned to me and said, 'Well, now are you satisfied? We'll be up here all night!'

I said to my wife, 'Treasure' – I always call her Treasure, she reminds me of something that's just been dug up.

Table manners

I took the wife to a restaurant last night. I said to the waiter, 'Do you serve crabs?'

He looked at the wife and said, 'We serve everybody.'

She did look a mess. She was wearing a white coat, white hat, and she'd put too much mascara on. She looked like an overweight panda with dropsy. I've never seen a woman eat so fast – she sits at the table with her elbows in starting blocks.

The wine waiter said, 'What would madam like to wash the meal down with?'

I said, 'I'm not sure but try Lake Windermere.'

I ordered a steak. I said to the waiter, 'Is it rare?'

He said, 'Judging by the look of it it's bloody near extinct.'

Just another day

Take an average day. I woke up at four o'clock this morning. The alarm was going off and a ginger camel was sitting at the dressing table. Straight away I knew something was wrong – because we never set the alarm for four. The wife was asleep with her mouth wide open. I bent across to kiss her, gently took the snooker cue from behind her ear and ran my finger down her duelling scar. I got up and put on my smoking jacket. By the time I got downstairs it was on fire – I wasn't bothered, it'll come in handy as a blazer.

I said to the chemist, 'Can I have some
sleeping pills for the wife?'
He said, 'Why?'
I said, 'She keeps waking up.'

My wife and I don't believe in not speaking.
We have our own special way of facing up to
and sorting out our differences – it's called
boxing.

Vengeance

At approximately two-thirty last Tuesday morning, a chilling mist rose from the garden of number 14 Herbal Terrace, Grimethorpe, the home of Ada and Alf Kipperwaithe. Ada was a hell of a size, a hard-bitten, bad tempered, muscular woman who dominated her skinny little husband, Alf.

That cold morning a burglar broke in the Kipperwaithes' house and pinched Ada's silver karate cups and some Goss china from an aunt in Bangor. Alf was on nights at the local Co-op when the police told him of the theft and that they'd caught the burglar. Alf marched into the police station and said, 'Where's the man who broke into my house?'

The desk sergeant paled at the menace in the little man's voice. Alf pushed him to one side, strode into the cells and grabbed a fellow through the bars and snarled, 'Are you the man who broke into my house while my dear wife was asleep?'

The burglar broke down. 'Don't hit me! Revenge isn't any good!'

'Leave that for the police,' said Alf. 'Here's £10, there's something you've got to tell me, and tell me now: how the hell did you get in without waking the wife up?'

My wife's got that classical look – she looks like Beethoven.

❋

They say you should always smile when you're poor. It's perfectly true. They've just rushed the wife to hospital, delirious with laughter.

❋

I found the wife's school report the other day. No wonder she'd hidden it. The teacher had written: 'All I can say of this girl is I'm sorry they abolished the death penalty.'

❋

She has a fear that one night in a dark street a sex maniac will jump out and ignore her.

> (PLAY — NOSE — RASP)
> ———— • ————
> YOU WON'T BELIEVE IT BUT I'VE BEEN
> PLAYING THE PIANO SINCE I WAS SIX
> YEARS OLD — THE TROUBLE IS I WAS TWENTY
> NINE BEFORE MY MOTHER OPENED THE LID.

My wife talks so much, she gets lip cramp.

People who know I'm henpecked say, 'Are
you a man or a mouse?'
Well, I must be a man because the wife's
frightened of mice.

'I never made love to my wife before I was
married. Did you?'
'I don't know. What was her maiden name?'

We had a goose for Christmas last year. The wife said, 'It's took me two days to cook it.'
I asked, 'Why?'
She said, 'Well it screams when you pull its feathers out.'

From fear, fortitude

The Tzar of Russia was so frightened when he saw Napoleon that the shock made him work harder for his country and, through his labour, he laid the foundation stone of the great modern Russia.

George Washington was so scared when he first looked at a Red Indian savage that his fear welded together the settlers to make America powerful and rich.

Bearing this fear in mind I did something yesterday that's bound to put this country back on its feet – I sent the Prime Minister a photograph of the wife. What a face! She's been on the Ten-Day Beauty Plan for five years …

She's had her face lifted so often she talks
through her naval.

Ours is a football marriage, we keep waiting
for the other one to kick off.

She once licked my cheek. I asked, 'Do you
love me?'
She replied, 'No I need the salt.'

I said, 'I could live in your eyes.'
She said, 'You'd be at home, there's a sty in
one of them.'

SPOT

NEARLY
I SOLD MY HOUSE LAST WEEK FOR ~~FIVE~~ FOUR
THOUSAND POUNDS — WHICH IS NT BAD CONSIDERING
THAT ONLY TWO YEARS AGO I PAID £6000
FOR IT... I PUT THE HOUSE IN THE HANDS OF AN
ESTATE AGENT — HE MADE IT SOUND SO NICE I
WENT OUT AND BOUGHT IT AGAIN

She was born under Taurus the Bull and it
trod on her …

✼

My wife's getting better at driving now.
It's got to the stage where the road begins to
turn at the same place as she does.

✼

She said, 'Will you love me when I'm old
and baggy?'
I said, 'Why worry about tomorrow?'

SCRIPT ONE.

"GOOD EVENING ≡ VERY NICE TO BE HERE — ANYWHERE REALLY IF ITS DRY: I DON'T GET MANY BOOKINGS WHEN YOU'VE SEEN ACT YOU'LL KNOW WHY ≡ NEARLY A YEAR SINCE LAST HERE ≡ HELL OF A LONG TIME TO BE OUT OF WORK ≡ ONE THING LIFE HAS TAUGHT ME — MONEY CAN'T BUY EVERYTHING — NOT CERTAIN FORMS OF EXTREME POVERTY: I HAVE LOST 14 JOBS THROUGH ILLNESS — THEY ALL GOT SICK OF ME:

— WILL PLAY MOVING PIECE ON PIANOFORTE WRITTEN FOR ME BY FRIEND WHO WROTE IT WHILST DYING — ON HUDDERSFIELD COMPOST HEAP DURING BARNSLEY EGG RIOTS AT ACTON — VERY SOMBRE CLASSIC — ♪ ♫ ♫

— THEN HE DIED:

— IF YOU'R WONDERING WHATS NEXT — DON'T ITS GOT ME BOTHERED AS WELL.

You should see her in a see-through nightie
– like a side of bacon in deep freeze.

My wife spends money like water.
Trouble is, I only earn it like treacle.

I'm not saying the wife's ugly, but last
Christmas she stood under the mistletoe
waiting for someone to kiss her ... and she
was still there at Lent.

I'm not saying the wife's ugly, but last

My wife sent her photograph to the Lonely
Hearts Club.
They sent it back saying they weren't that
lonely.

She went to the pictures to see *Dracula* – the
audience thought she was making a personal
appearance.

My wife is 38-26-38. That's only her neck.

She's so bald that when she goes to a bowling alley, people put their fingers up her nose.

The wife threw coffee on the floor.
That's grounds for divorce.

She's so cross eyed that when she cries tears
run down her back.

Her teeth stick out so much it looks as if
her nose is playing a piano.

She's got a complexion like a peach – yellow
and fuzzy.

My wife has said that she's fed up with
so much sex on the telly. The trouble is,
she keeps getting the aerial wire tangled
round her legs ... it'd be worse if we had
an indoor aerial ...

❀

She's got a complexion like a peach – yellow
and fuzzy.

❀

And she's got so many double chins it looks
as though she's leaning her head on a pile of
crumpets.

ALL IN A
DAY'S
WORK

You might not know this, but I started my
career singing in the streets.
I was so bad they threw me into the nearest
theatre.

I'm not in very good shape. I used to have broad
shoulders and a deep chest – but that's all behind
me now. I went to give a pint of blood last week.
They pumped for an hour then settled for a gill.

Thank you for that sparse ripple of enthusiasm
when I came on. I'm grateful because last
week at the El Tropicana Club in Goole, the silence
that greeted my act was so intense that the mere
shifting of a wine gum from one tooth to another
reverberated like a musket volley.

Beethoven's eldest brother...

I had intended to commence my pianoforte recital by playing you a little something of Mozart's – but I won't, because he never plays any of mine. Then I toyed with the idea of playing a snatch from Ravel's 'Pavane pour une infante défunte', but the only trouble is I can't remember now if it is a tune or a Latin prescription for chilblains. So instead I'd like to play a beautiful composition written by Beethoven's eldest brother Syd, who wrote it as he lay dying after an accident at the St Alban's fish festival.

People often ask me how I manage to keep so jolly and full of zip – it isn't always easy.

The mother-in-law lives with us, you know. She came about three weeks ago – I remember the day well because next door's savage Alsatian was whimpering.

Anyway, I awoke, did my morning exercises – up, one, two, three. Down, one, two, three. Then my other eyelid. I kissed the wife gently on her black eye patch, she stirred and for one dreadful moment, with her having no teeth in, it was like peering down the open end of a damp euphonium. It's hard to describe the wife first thing in the morning, but a fortnight ago she undressed without drawing the bedroom curtains and a peeping Tom across the road gave himself up. She tries so hard to be beautiful; she's had her face lifted so often that in the future they'll have to lower her body. She's not got a bad figure, except when she wears a mini-skirt she looks like a badly chipped drop leaf table.

❉

I've tried hard to get on … pubs, clubs, theatres, they're all excellent sources of unemployment to me.

❉

I can't manage. I'm so far behind with the mortgage repayments that the arrears are written in Latin.

Insects

I once played in a place called the Tropicana club, Scunthorpe. It was under a viaduct in the attic of a blouse factory. They had a bouncer on the door throwing drunks in. What an audience! If they liked your act they didn't clap, they let you live.

The digs I had were the worst I'd never been in. the landlady must have come from North Wales –

At least, she had a face like flint. The house was filthy – the windows were cleaned with a Brillo Pad and the carpets were so dirty the beetles walked across them on stilts. The landlady's husband once hung his stocking up at Christmas and the tree died.

The first day I was there I asked where the toilet was – the landlady said it was outside in the garden. I went down a weed-choked path full of nettles and groundsel. The toilet was a horror – flies, bluebottles, wasps, hornets. I fled back to the house. I said, 'Dreadful – that toilet is full of ghastly insects!'

She said, 'You should use it at dinnertime; they're all in the kitchen then!'

I used to work in a bicarbonate factory – I was a sort of relief worker. It did me till I got wind of something else.

A musical interlude

I'd like to play for you a haunting madrigal that I had the great distinction of presenting recently to the President of the United State ... Owned Laundries at the Friends of the Mafia Hot Pot Supper at the Hide and Skin Works, Wigan.

It was written under tragic circumstances for me by a great friend of mine who wrote it as he lay dying after falling headfirst into a barrel of kosher rum. Then he died.

It's a haunting tune and whenever I play it I think of her – my first love – and the last time we met in that dimly lit Hungarian gypsy restaurant in Crewe. I remember we were holding hands under the table – it took some doing, it was fourteen foot long. We hadn't enjoyed the meal, in fact I sent the caviar back twice because it smelt fishy. By the light of a candle on the table I saw my beloved's lips trembling. I bent across to kiss them, she snatched her head away angrily and it took fifteen minutes to get the wick from up my nose. She left and I never saw her again. I've often wondered what happened to Gladys Cottersbotham ...

It's a funny name, but you can't always judge things by names. Where we live all the hoses have names. There's one across the road that's called 'La Casa Romantica' – it's a two up two down and the drains are blocked. What a family! I met the dad the other day. He was out with so many kids! I said to him, 'If you have another youngster you'll have a football team.'

He said, 'I've got a football team, these are the reserves.'

I've only been in their house once. There were so many wet nappies in the kitchen there was a rainbow in the lobby.

Some of the neighbours put on airs and graces. One house on our side is called 'The Heights'. It's about a foot higher than ours – it was built on a tip. They never have Cream Crackers at their house, always *Crème de Crackeur*. His wife won at bingo last week. She didn't shout 'House!', she stood up, waved her gloves and shouted 'Maisonette!' The wife's calling our house 'Sonata', because with the cost of living nowadays we'll soon be doing a Moonlight.

❈

When I auditioned for Bernard Delfont his cigar ash burned my neck. He couldn't help it, I was kissing his feet at the time.

If success breeds success, then I must be on the pill.

For two years I toured with the Sadler Wells Ballet Company – I was the van driver.

I nearly didn't make it. My brother swallowed a live bullet. The doctor gave him a quart of castor oil. Dangerous? Only if you point him at anybody.

I had three setbacks this week – stereo, TV, radio.

Some say he's the funniest man in the country … I wouldn't know, I've never been to Peru.

❄

Unemployment is terrible where I live. The local paper had an advert for a nightclub croupier – first in the queue was the vicar.

❄

Making friends and meeting people

I'm always happy when I'm making friends and meeting people. Meeting people, that's what life's all about. I was in my local pub the other night. It's called The Dumb Fortnight because the beer's two weak for words. I said to the landlord, 'This beer's flat, warm and full of sediment.'

He said, 'You're lucky. You've only got a pint of it. I've got a bloody cellar full.'
At the back stood a chap on his own playing darts. A little fellow came in and stood next to him.

'Don't I know you?' the fellow said.

'I don't think so.'

'It'll come to me,' said the first chap. 'I've got it! We sheltered in an Alpine hut to escape an avalanche on the Matterhorn.'

The big fellow said no.

'Got it! We used to go shark fishing together off the Great Barrier Reef with a nymphomaniac pearl diver. She ran off with a Mexican evangelist and lost her knee cap in a bakery fire.'

The big fellow said no.

The little bloke said, 'It'll come to me … Wait a minute. We escaped from a prisoner of war camp in Upper Silesia. We were disguised as German barbers and we blew up a troop train with a hand grenade made to look like a rissole. We got into Holland and hid in a shed full of tulips until the war was over …'

The big man said no.

'Was you in here last night?' said the little bloke.

'Yes.'

'Well that's where I've seen you.'

❋

When I started I was the only comic to have been thrown out of places I hadn't even worked at.

At one time he had ambitions to be a sex maniac – but he failed his practical.

There was a big fire at our local income tax office last night but they put the blaze out before any serious good was done.

Have you seen the new tax form? It's very simple, just two questions:
(A) How much do you earn?
(B) Send it.

I'm still so poor, if I wrote a blank cheque it would bounce.

I was playing piano. Someone shouted, 'Get him off!'

The manager shouted, 'No, he's 'armless!'

I heard somebody say, 'That's what he ought to be ...'

✱

I've died more times than James Cagney ever did.

✱

I've not always been a comedian. There was a time when I had regular meals.

✱

My suit's so thin moths use it as a diet sheet.

When it comes to humour, people often ask me, 'What's the difference between a northern audience and a southern audience?' Frankly, as far as I'm concerned there's no difference – they don't laugh at me in the South either. The reason I work for Yorkshire TV is that they're so good to me. They can never do enough for me – so they don't bother trying …

I've been on the dole so often, whenever they build a new labour exchange they call me in as a consultant.

When I write a letter to the income tax people, I always drink a bottle of scotch – after all two heads are better than one.

Money

Speaking of money, it's not been a happy time for me. I received a final demand from the tax man last week. I could tell I owed a lot because on the front of the envelope was written Chapter One … I'm also behind with my mortgage repayments – well, I must be 'cos the Building Society is holding the wife hostage.

I went to see the bank manager to try and get a loan. I said, 'How does my account stand?'

He said, 'I'll toss you for it.'

We sat down in his office. He said, 'Mr Dawson, have you got any collateral?'

I said, 'No, it's just the way my legs are crossed.'

He said, 'You've been coming to this bank now for seven years and you've never noticed that I've got a glass eye.'

I said, 'It's your left one.'

He said, 'How did you know?'

I said, 'It's the only one with a spark of humanity in it.'

The trouble these days is you just don't get value for your money. I went to a West End tailor for a suit. I said, 'What can I have for twenty-five pounds?'

He gave me some wool and a loom.

I bought a second-hand car last year. The

salesman said, 'You'll get a lot of pleasure out of it.' And he was right – it's a pleasure to get out of it. I don't know how old it is but you have to start it with a whip. It must be the only car on the road with thatched tyres.

I was in show business for years. Fortunately now I'm making a living.

I stayed at the Fiddle Hotel – what a vile-inn …

I was in a play on the TV once. It was one of those suspense plays. It kept you wondering … what's on the other channels?

Always on the go

One of the moving stories I ever heard was in a senna pod factory. I was a foreman on the conveyor belt and I was always on the go. One night I got invited to a Scrabble party at a teetotallers' coming of age. I was halfway through a carrot cocktail (they're very good: you still get drunk but you see better) when there was a knock at the door. I went with my hostess to open it, and stood on the doorstep was an old tramp. He said, 'Missus, last week you gave me a waistcoat and in the pocket I found two £5 notes.'

She said, 'You honest man! You've brought the money back!'

He said, 'No, I've come for another waistcoat!'

People say to me, 'Cheer up! Lady Luck will smile on you one day.' By the time she smiles on me she won't have any teeth left.

151

Comedians run in my family – they have to.

Good fortune has passed me by so many
times that I walk along the road giving a
slow down signal.

I can't tell you how happy I am to be here –
If I was a liar I could.

Whatever I earn is going towards a worthy cause,
and that is to send my wife and her mother to the
country … India, Burma, Tibet … anywhere will
do.

Master criminal

When I was a Detective Inspector in the Dorset CID I found myself up against a master criminal who called himself, oh, what was it? Let me see, he was brown and sounded like a bell … Ah, yes, that was his name: Dung. He used to lurk in a thicket and jump out on women and make love to them while singing 'Old McDonald Had a Farm'.

We knew he had one weakness – a fondness for roast pork and curried prunes.

One night, disguised as a Turkish knife-grinder's concubine and with a pig under each arm, I set out to trap the fiend. Halfway across a field I met a farmer's daughter called Daisy – so named because she grew wild in the woods.

'Oi'll walk with 'e in case 'e get attacked,' I said.

'Wait a mo, you might attack me!'

'How could I attack you with two pigs under my arms?'

'Easy, if I was to hold them for you.'

I used to be known as 003 – licensed to strangle hernias.

Good evening. First of all, let me thank you for the wonderful reception you gave me this evening. Not only for the one just now but for the one you gave me earlier outside when I was busking the queue.

✶

What amazes me is that so many people think show business is glamorous and exciting. Believe me, it's about as glamorous as changing the sheets in a bed-wetting clinic.

✶

Did you hear about the TV executive who made a marvellous speech to his staff about having an economy drive? It was so effective they gave him two cheers.

✶

I was a spy in the Bank of England – I was a mint spy.

People keep away from me. I'm tough, fast with a gun and I've got BO.

In fact I was born with a shotgun on my knee. Hell of a job to put my trousers on.

I'm about as well known as Lord Godiva.

I'm good at karate – I once broke a plank
with my head – just like that, concussion.

And the women – Raquel Welch, Bridget
Bardot, Gladys Alcock – that's the one I went
out with.

I went to my doctor and asked for
something for persistent wind. He gave me a
kite.

I went to my office the other day and a
nut fell on my head. I thought, 'Nice one,
squirrel.'

A lot of people believe that show business consists of all-night parties and sex orgies. Well, the nearest I've got to an orgy was when the au pair's garter snapped at Scrabble.

❉

Spinning Margaret

Good evening ladies and gentlemen. I didn't expect thunderous applause when my name was announced – and I wasn't far wrong, either. I'm not surprised. My Great Aunt Margaret, just before she passed away at the ripe old age of ninety-eight, beckoned me to her side and whispered, 'Nephew, if you ever fail to get a laugh as a comedian I'll turn over in my grave.'

I attended a séance in Birmingham recently, the medium went into a deep trance and said, 'I don't know who this message is for, but I'm getting a very strange message through from somebody called Spinning Margaret ...'

She was the last of the Gaiety Girls in Edwardian London; men drank Champagne from her slipper and threw roses at her as she danced. She was fifty-nine when she retired, with damp feet and greenfly.

Despite her foreboding I'm doing pretty well. I'm

booked here tonight; I've a booking for next August – and one for the following March. Trouble is, they're not just engagements, to me that's a career. People keep saying, 'Don't worry, Les. Success is just around the corner!' Which is not very encouraging as I live on the M1.

Fortunately, I don't rely on doing this sort of thing for a living. I'm only doing it so I can purchase a few luxuries for my family at Christmas ... just little luxuries like bread and cheese ...

If I ever get worried I do like they say in the song, 'Grab your coat and get your hat, leave your worries on the doorstep ...' Our house is the only one in the street with a doorstep twelve feet high.

I was working at the Copacabana, Scunthope and this man approached me after the show. He said, 'I were watching your act from behind the snooker table. Are you approachable?' I said 'Yes.' He said, 'Can I give you a word of constructive criticism?' I said, 'Certainly.' He said, 'I think you're crap.'

I may look overweight but my doctor assures me that for my age I'm exactly the right weight – though I should be twelve inches taller. So he put me on a diet. I can eat anything I want – bread, potatoes, cakes, anything. But I mustn't swallow it.

❀

'Since his last appearance on this show we've received two thousand letters asking him to come back ... and any man who can afford two thousand stamps deserves to come back ...'

❀

ACKNOWLEDGEMENTS

Thanks to Louise Dixon, George Maudsley, Madeleine Ovenden, Ed Lomas, Greg Stevenson and Ron Callow for all their help in editing illustrating and designing this book.